# YOUR ORDER IS IN THE FIRE

By:
Apostle Lisa Exum

Copyright 2018 by Elle Ruach Media Group, LLC

ISBN: 978-1-945304-29-3

All rights reserved.

No part of this book may be reproduced in any manner whatsoever without written permission except in the case of brief quotations embodied in critical articles and reviews.

Cover and Interior Design & Layout: PricelessDigitalMedia.com

# DEDICATION

I would like to dedicate this book to my four amazing children: Hosea, Sloan, Tiffany, and Tabitha. Apart from Jesus, you are so precious to me. I am inspired to leave you this legacy. You are my hidden treasures. Each one of you are a treasure, precious and rare. You are not perfect; yet you are my treasure. Thank you for always encouraging me. I love you with all my heart. May you continue to walk in the anointing which the Lord has called you.

I also want to dedicate this book to my two grandchildren, A'niya and Jeremiah. My endless joy.

# ACKNOWLEDGEMENT

First and foremost, I want to thank my Lord Jesus Christ to whom I give all the glory, all the honor, and all the praise. It is truly a blessing that the Lord gave me the vision for this book.

I Love You, Jesus! ♥

**Let All Things Be Done Decently And In Order.**

~1 Corinthians 14:40

# CONTENTS

**INTRODUCTION** ........................................................................... 9

**CHAPTER ONE**    KEEP PRAYING ...................................................... 13

**CHAPTER TWO**    WHICH WAY DO I GO? ........................................ 19

**CHAPTER THREE** IMAGE OF GOD .................................................... 21

**CHAPTER FOUR**   CHARACTERISTICS OF GODLY WOMEN ...... 25

**CHAPTER FIVE**   GODLY MEN OF ORDER .................................... 29

**CHAPTER SIX**    TRIALS OF FIRE ................................................... 35

**CHAPTER SEVEN** FOUR AREAS OF TESTING ............................... 51

# INTRODUCTION

Are you having trouble understanding God's divine order, and what He wants to accomplish through you? God wants to show you what it takes to walk into your divine destiny and purpose. He loves you so much that He thought it important to show you what it takes to reach your divine destiny.

God has given me a mandate to write this book, to teach the people of God what it takes to walk in divine order, because there are so many Christian people struggling with their purpose in life. I believe that after you read this book, your mind will be at ease. The impartation from this book will bring about a change in your thinking, to empower and transform your spiritual life. It will change your life. It will help transition you into your divine destiny. You will begin to understand what it is that God is trying to do in you.

God wants to reveal four principles of divine order, to empower and transform your spiritual life. The four principles are faith, humility, obedience, and integrity. Many people have no idea where to start, or what to do to start, serving God. There is much frustration and confusion about who they are. When God called many of you to serve in ministry, you struggled with who you are in God. You don't know what to do, or where to start. It can be overwhelming and just plain scary. The trials that God put you through will build Christ-like character, so that you can build a foundation in Christ. God's process will bring clarity to all that you have been through in your life and your time of testing. The things you go through prepare you for ministry. There are so many struggles to reaching your divine destiny. You struggle with what God is doing. Sometimes you ask, *"How can all of this work out for the good of God?"*. It seems impossible because of the pain that you have endured. The struggles that come with the trials can be so painful and agonizing. Just thinking back to what I endured makes me cringe. I have come to understand that the process was real.

We sometimes think to ourselves, *"Why would God want to use me?"* You may think you are no good to yourself, nor to anyone else. Maybe you think you can't do this. I used to think, *"Where will I get the strength to do what God has called me to do. How will I do it?"* This process requires order. You must go through the fire to be purified. Purification is needed to bring divine order into your life. As you walk in divine order, you will come to know God in a real way. Only God can process you to bring divine order into your life. Let's take a look at what you need to do to get started. You should always pray about everything. Prayer will get you in the place you need to be. I hear a lot of people saying that they have to get themselves together before coming to God. There is nothing to do but just come to God in prayer. For those of you that are not Christian believers, you must first believe that God is real. Then, you must receive the gift of salvation.

There is nothing for you to do before you receive salvation. In order to receive salvation, you must first believe that Jesus is Lord and Savior, and that Jesus died on the cross for your sins.

Romans 10:8-13(NKJV) — "But what does it say? The word is near you; it is in your mouth and in your heart, that is, the word of faith we are proclaiming: [9] That if you confess with your mouth, Jesus is Lord, and believe in your heart that God raised him from the dead, you will be saved. [10] For it is with your heart that you believe and are justified, and it is with your mouth that you confess and are saved. [11] As the Scripture says, anyone who trusts in him will never be put to shame. [12] For there is no difference between Jew and Gentile - the same Lord is Lord of all and richly blesses all who call on him, [13] For, everyone who calls on the name of the Lord will be saved."

## PRAYER OF SALVATION

Heavenly Father, I come to you. I acknowledge you as God, Creator of Heaven and Earth. Father, I confess that I am a sinner; I have sinned against you. I believe in my heart that Jesus Christ is your Son, and you sent your son to Earth, and he was born of a virgin.

I believe that Jesus Christ is the one true sacrifice for my sins.

I believe that Jesus Christ was crucified on a cross as a sacrifice for the sins of the world, sins which have separated me from you.

I believe, Heavenly Father, that you sent Jesus Christ to personally die for me and my sins.

I believe Jesus Christ, your son, took upon himself all of my sins and the sins of all mankind.

I believe Jesus, who knew no sin, became sin for me that I may receive eternal life.

I believe, Heavenly Father, you raised Jesus Christ from the dead, and he is alive and well, seated at the right hand in Heaven. I now repent and turn from my sins and choose to follow and obey Christ Jesus as my Lord and Savior. I ask you, Jesus Christ, to be the Lord of my life and lead me in all areas of my life. I receive you, Lord Jesus, as my Lord and Savior with all my heart and believe that you are my King and my God.

Lord, fill me with your Holy Spirit, and use my life as a willing vessel. Heavenly Father, I ask that my life will glorify you.

Thank you, Heavenly Father, for my salvation by faith in Christ Jesus and the Truth of Your Word, in Jesus Name. Amen!

If you have prayed this prayer, you are now saved! Praise God! Hallelujah! Glory to God! Now, go find a church to serve God! Amen!

This takes us back to prayer. God will seek you out. He will reveal Himself to you in a way that there will be no mistaking that He is talking to you. He knows your name. He is calling you. So don't ignore the call, because the process is real. The four principles that God uses to transform your life can and will shake up your life. You might ask, "Will I get through this?" The answer is YES! Your fiery trials and tests are designed just for you and only you.

Jeremiah 1:5(NKJV) — "Before I formed you in the womb, I knew you; before you were born I set you apart. I appointed you as a prophet to the nations." ~JUST KEEP PRAYING

# CHAPTER ONE

## KEEP PRAYING
*1 Thess.5:17 – "Pray Without Ceasing."*

One thing about me is this: I have always been true to myself. What I am saying is that, you have to just be who you are. You can't fake it until you make it. I always tell people that there is nothing we can do to be righteous. The righteousness of God comes from God only. God is the only one that can make us righteous (James 2:21-24). I say this because I remember being out there in the world. I had no idea about order. I got saved, and I tried to stop doing everything all at once. Boy, was that a mess! It felt like I had been buried alive. That was the most horrible feeling. I thought I had to be perfect. Instead, it was flesh fighting against righteousness.

So, I figured I would stop going out partying. That did not work at all. I realized that I was trying to do something that was impossible for me. Flesh cannot help us get into divine order. But, all things are possible with God (Philippians 4:13). After that experience, I learned that I could not do it on my own. But, nothing is impossible with Christ Jesus. I put it in the hands of God. I can remember telling people to live their life and when God is ready for them to be righteous and holy, it will happen. God's plan for your life will work itself out. By the grace of God, and only God. When I submitted myself to God, God saw me righteous. He was working in me so that He could show up in me (Romans 8:1). I was made whole. My order was being processed. The fire of God was working in me. It was burning up everything that was not of God and making me more like Jesus.

As a figure of speech, when I straddled the fence, it was hard to try and live righteously. Straddling the fence meant "not being able to decide whether or not I would live by God's law or do what I wanted to do." I was praying and still living the worldly life. I was going to church on Sunday and partying in the club on the weekend. I thought the weekends were my time. I was doing what I wanted to do on the weekend. I wasn't much of a drinker, but I loved to dance. I loved music! Lord, knows I had to keep praying. I prayed all the time. I did not know what else to do. I had no clue about righteousness and living Holy. I thought I had to get it right. I had to keep praying. It was important that I stayed consistent, so I kept praying. The Word of God tells us to pray without ceasing (1 Thess. 5:17). When we pray without ceasing, we pray about everything. We give God total control of our life, and we go to God about everything concerning our lives.

It may not seem important, but something as simple as what to wear can make all the difference in your day. Many things that seem insignificant to us are very important to the Lord. I know someone is reading this and thinking, *"What in the world?"* Or, *"This is me right here."* Some of you are still partying. And, you are so far away from God that you can't seem to grasp the hand of God no matter what you do. You pray sometimes. Then, you go to church, and you are still no closer to God. Then, you think, *"What must I do to get to you, Lord?"* You might even say, *"Maybe there is hope for me, too."* I will say this, God will not turn His back on you (Hebrews 13:5). God will lead you down the path of righteousness. If you back-slide, pick yourself up, and keep moving forward. No one is perfect and no one has arrived. Our inadequate behavior and faults mean nothing to the one that has created us. He uses every bit of what we have been through to help someone else.

Once I had been a disciple under God for a period of time, my character started to change. I was starting to be more like Christ. God will disciple you personally. I knew that it was time for something more. I literally ate the words of God. There were many experiences with God. Some of my experiences did not seem like they actually happened, but it was all a part of God developing my character to be more like Jesus. I still did not know who I was, but God was raising me up to know who I was in Him. He was making me. Once I had been transformed, things started to change for my good and for the good of every soul connected to me. I was God's prophet, His messenger. I am not saying that things were perfect, but when you have God fighting for you, things just work out better than you could ever think or imagine. Sometimes we have to get it wrong in order to get it right. If you don't know what you did wrong, how will you know what you have done right.

Everything that we go through has purpose. Even when we don't know what it means, just keep praying and pray about everything. Sometimes, we have to go through some things in order to get to where we want to be. We have to posture ourselves. This is the place you want to be. The place where it all seems to make sense. Prayer can go places you cannot be physically. Posture is positioning yourself to receive from the Lord. God taught me to posture myself in prostrating before God. Prostrating means lying on your face; it is a humbling oneself. Humility is where God wants us to be in order to receive from Him. After you have gone through all the hurt and pain, you feel like there has to be more to God. You come this far and you want to know, which way do I go now? And you hear the voice of God saying, "Come this way." Psalm 32:8 – "God gives us divine counsel. He instructs us which way to go. God will lead us on a path of right understanding."

Isaiah 30:21 – "Your ears shall hear a word behind you, saying, 'This is the way, walk in it.'" Whenever you turn to the right hand or whenever you turn to the left, God will guide you and give you direction. The Lord will light your path if you allow him."

People are creatures of habit. We want to do things the way we want to do them. But, God will have his way no matter the way we start and finish. God's way is life changing. He will teach us the right way to go (Ps.25:8, NKJV). And the process is transforming you, to empower you, to get your life in order. There is only one way to do this. It is by divine order. God's ways are not our ways, and His thoughts are not our thoughts (Jer. 29:11). He wants us to walk in divine order so that we develop the character of Jesus.

When the Holy Spirit envelops your life, you have no choice but to get right with God. The hand of God is forever moving. And the fire of God will burn up everything that is not right in our lives. The hand of God is the fire of God. The fire of God brings order into our lives. Being molded by the hand of God must become our all consuming fire. It changes us. We are transformed by the fire of God. It causes us to come into divine order. We are transformed by the renewing of our minds (Romans 12:2). We must have a change of heart, so to speak. We have to stop doing the things that we are doing that are not right. Worldly things grieve the Holy Spirit. If you know the Lord, you should be convicted by the things you do that are not of God. REPENT! The kingdom of Heaven is at hand (Matt.3:2). Stop doing evil! Ask God to forgive you of your sins and stop doing the wrong that you do. It is not a game anymore. It's time to get right with God. I knew that I had to stop all the nonsense. Because once you are saved, God expects more from you. You can't keep slipping up, especially if you are called to ministry. There is no excuse. So, you have to keep praying.

As you posture yourself in prayer, God will start to reveal himself to you. God is revealed through his glory. When we go through, and it doesn't seem to be changing, then suddenly something happens and things start to change. This is God's glory. God's glory is the kabod of Heaven. Once you have reached a level of prayer within the kabod, things will literally open up to you as you are flowing in God's majestic power. This happens when your prayer life gets stronger. You have to keep praying so that you don't miss your season. Each season is new and filled with new mercies, new blessings, new dimensions, and new glories. Just keep praying. God is sure to answer your every prayer. Pray because you don't want to miss what God has for you.

Like Dr. Juanita Standifer Woodson said, "God is about to pour out a new glory."

Imagine this: you are walking up to this huge door, and you start knocking. The sound is the echo of years to come. You are knocking on time. Every prayer is a moment in time. God hears your prayers. God knows what you need before you even ask or before you even begin to think of it. When you pray, you are knocking on God's heart. Every prayer is the heartbeat of God. God knows what you have need of. So, just keep praying.

Have you ever noticed how things change in time? God does a shifting, and the domino effect causes the things that you prayed for years ago to come to past. It's important that you always pray. No matter what happens, just continue to pray. We must pray constantly. God's timing is not our timing. In our time, things seem to stand still; but in God's time, things are constantly moving swiftly when a shifting takes place. During a shift, at the appointed time, prayers get answered. God is sure to answer your prayers. Everything you say to God will come back to you. Remember that God answers prayers according to his timing. God answers our prayers according to the time table set of Heaven.

God's timetable is set according to what is placed before him. Sometimes we pray amiss and prayers get trapped in the atmosphere of confusion. Many prayers are snatched up by the enemy's help. The enemy will steal and delay our prayers so that he can attempt to stop what God is doing or going to do. The enemy cannot stop what God is doing. You are the only one that can stop your blessing. Be clear about what you say to God, because God needs us to be transparent when we pray. God will always reveal which way to go through our process of prayer. Pray about everything because God is a revealing God

(Daniel 2:47). No matter what is happening, just keep praying. Because whatever is happening in the natural realm, is not what is happening in the spiritual realm. God is a faithful God (Deut. 7:9). He keeps His promises. That is why it's so important that we pray all the time. We should set aside some time every day to pray. Take some time to come before the Lord in prayer. We are to pray without ceasing. Keep the issues that we have before the Lord in prayer daily. Daily prayer will help in our direction. Prayer helps direct our path. It also helps keep you in covenant with God. Also, when you pray all the time, you will have a direct contact with God. There won't be no long wait to get a prayer through. God will answer you immediately.

# CHAPTER TWO

## WHICH WAY DO I GO?

*Psalm 32:8 – "I will instruct you and teach you in the way you should go;
I will guide you with my eye."*

As a little girl, my life was very emotional. Many of you can identify with this. When you are born with a prophetic spirit, you are more sensitive to things in the atmosphere. At a very young age— of about six years old— God started talking to me. He began to give me very vivid dreams. Some will read this and think to themselves that this is not true. Well, don't take my word for it. I was chosen (Num.16:5). Trust the Lord, your God, to reveal Himself to you as you seek Him. God was taking me places in my visions and dreams that I am sure no man had yet gone.

I remember speaking in tongues. I knew it was something, but what was it? Yes, I was a dreamer. I was often reminded that I was a dreamer. My mother worked hard to do all that she could humanly do, but I still always had a knowing that there was something missing. I was right! Mommy worked hard to raise us, but I was somehow different. Out of all my siblings, I seemed to be more sensitive than the others. I was always crying. I always had a longing for more. I was a peculiar child. 1 Peter 2:9 (KJV)— "But ye are a chosen generation, a royal priesthood, a holy nation, a peculiar people; that ye should shew forth the praises of him who hath called you out of darkness into his marvelous light."

The old folks called it 'peculiar'. My grandmother would take me to church, and I felt like I was at home. It was an old Baptist church. Grandma would get happy (in other words, the spirit of God would be upon her). God would be with me, too. Grandma told me that I was a very wise child. I used to spend hours talking to my grandfather. Yes, I was very wise. I was wise because God was with me. I love Jesus! I attended an all-girl private Catholic school. But, even during that time, God always walked and talked with me. I mentioned the private school because it doesn't matter where you start as long as you stay on the path to your destiny. God will order your steps at a very young age. The Bible says, "train up a child in the way he should go, and when he is old, he will not depart from it." (Proverbs 22:6). God was with me. He knew the way I would go. God ordered my steps! Psalm 37:23 – "The steps of a good man are ordered by the Lord, and he delights in his way." God delights in the person that follows Him, trusts Him, and tries to do His will. God watches over every step that we take. When a man's ways are right and pleasing, God will be with him.

God was with me. Just like He will be with you as you ask Him which way to go. Seek God for your direction. Let me show you the way that God took me on my journey of transformation to my destiny. God's ways are not our ways. Our ways are never going to be the ways of anyone else. Everyone has their own plan designed by God. A man's ways can be complicated.

Especially, if we do not follow the plan that God has laid out for us to follow. Sometimes, we get upset, and we may even be confused as we try to figure out which way to go. But, take heart. Don't give up and throw in the towel (Gal.6:9, KJV).

The path that leads to righteousness can be hard, frustrating, and complicated. But, it can also be rewarding – provided that we keep our minds stayed on Jesus. Keep praying and continue to seek the Lord for direction. Never quit!

# CHAPTER THREE

## IMAGE OF GOD

*Genesis 5:1, In the day that God created man,*
*He made him in the likeness of God*

God has a purpose and a plan for your life. Jeremiah 29:11 – "God knows the plans He has for you. God plans to prosper you and not cause you harm. He has a hope and a future for you. He gives each of us a divine plan. God will teach you how to be a man or woman of divine destiny! Women are the expressed image of God. God uses the woman as a powerful vessel."

In the beginning, God created the Heavens and the Earth(Gen.1:1). Our destiny was already laid out before we were created. Genesis 1:3 – "God said let there be light; and there was light." In other words, let there be order. Light represents truth being revealed. Nothing is hidden from light (owr). In Hebrew, (owr) light exposes darkness. The hidden things are revealed and exposed. Light sets things in order. Light exposes disorder. So therefore, we need light to set things in order. Destiny is fulfilled by walking through darkness to come into the light. As we walk through darkness, we will begin to see the light. We need light to see where we are going. Light reveals the things that are hidden.

Genesis 1:26 – "God created man in the image of God. God already knew that He needed someone to manage all that He had created in the Earth." Then God said, "[26] Let us make man in our image, according to our likeness; let them have dominion over the fish of the sea, over the birds of the air, and over the cattle, over all the Earth, and over every creeping thing that creeps on the Earth. 27 So God created man in His own image; in the image of God, He created them; male and female."

But then, God looked and wanted to add to His creation. God loved us so much that He had to bring woman up out of man.

In Gen. 2:22 — "Then, the rib which the Lord God had taken from man, He made into a woman, and He brought her to the man. 23 And Adam said: '"This is now bone of my bones

And flesh of my flesh;

She shall be called Woman, because she was taken out of Man (Gen. 2:22-23)."

And so God created a woman. God took her from the rib of man. A woman will bring more light into this garden. God in his infinite being, already purposed in His mind for woman to come forth. The woman was already whole and the perfect fit for the man. A woman is already complete. She lacks nothing. The very essence of a woman is strength. She is a force to be reckoned with. A woman will fight to protect what she has knowledge of. She will protect what comes out of her. As man should protect a woman.

"For a man, indeed, ought not to cover his head, since he is the image and glory of God; but woman is the glory of man(1 Cor.11:7)." God had to create a woman to get man to bring order to all that God had created. A godly woman is like a fire that kindles a man's purpose. She will help a man set his life in order.

## EMPOWERMENT PRAYER

Heavenly Father, I come to you with repentance in my heart.

Lord, I ask that you forgive me for anything that I have said, done, or thought that is not like you.

Lord, anything that is not like you, I ask that you remove it from me. You are Jehovah Jireh, my provider, the God that supplies all my needs according to your riches and glory.

Lord, you are Jehovah Gibbor, you are mighty in battle, you said you would fight against them that fight against me.

Lord, you said that no weapon formed against me shall prosper, and every tongue that rises against me in judgment you shall condemn. This is the heritage of the servants of the Lord, and their righteousness is from you Lord (Isa.54:17).

Lord, you said, "Is not my word like a fire? And like a hammer that breaks the rock in pieces" (Jer.23:29)?

Lord, empower me, direct my path and show me the way to go. Let the fire of God move in my life.

Lord, let your fire purify me and make me whole. I overcome all obstacles that would block my path and come to eat up my blessings. Greater is He that is in me, than He that is in the world (1 John 4:4).

Lord, open my mind and give me clear vision to see your divine plan that you have for me and my life.

Lord, transform my mind and give me greater understanding to do your divine will. Let faith stand up in me. Clothe me in humility. According to Ephesians 3:13, I declare that I will not lose heart during my tribulations.

Lord, give me integrity to show me what is the right thing to do. Help me to walk in obedience, so that I may walk in divine order.

I take authority of every evil spirit that would come to block the plans for my life.

Lord, pour out your spirit upon me and grace me with supernatural knowledge and supernatural wisdom. I decree that I am empowered so that I may be strengthened and declare that I am enlightened and enabled to do the will of God.

Lord, I love you, I praise you, I give you honor. I praise your Holy name.

Lord, I thank you, and I give you all the praise and all the honor. In Jesus' name Amen!

# CHAPTER FOUR

## CHARACTERISTICS OF GODLY WOMEN

How do you know if you are chosen? We have distinct characteristics of our former brothers and sisters in Christ. Women have many characteristics. They are positioned in God to do great and mighty things. Women are known to be courageous as they press towards their destiny. However, they may have thrown in the towel from time to time.

God is a God of order. God is looking for a woman who is notable. God is looking for a remnant of women that have the characteristics of divine order. There were many women in the Bible that were worthy of being noticed. Today, God is still looking for notable women. Here, I have mentioned some of God's chosen vessels:

**1. Eve,: The First Woman of God (The woman of curiosity):**

"So when the woman saw that the tree was good for food, that it was pleasant to the eyes, and a tree desirable to make one wise, she took of its fruit and ate. She also gave to her husband with her, and he ate (Gen.3:6)."

**2. Hagar,: The Discarded Woman (Wife):**

"[14] So Abraham rose early in the morning and took bread and a skin of water, and putting it on her shoulder, he gave it and the boy to Hagar, and sent her away. Then, she departed and wandered in the wilderness of Beersheba. [15] And the water in the skin was used up, and she placed the boy under one of the shrubs. ¹⁶ Then, she went and sat down across from him at a distance of about a bowshot; for she said to herself, "Let me not see the death of the boy." So, she sat opposite him, and lifted her voice and wept. ¹⁷ And God heard the voice of the lad. Then, the angel of God called to Hagar out of Heaven, and said to her. What ails you, Hagar? Fear not, for God has heard the voice of the lad where he is. ¹⁸ "Arise, lift up the lad and hold him with your hand, for I will make him a great nation." ¹⁹ Then, God opened her eyes, and she saw a well of water. And she went and filled the skin with water, and gave the lad a drink (Gen. 21:14-19)."

### 3. Miriam,: The Ambitious Woman:

"Then Miriam and Aaron spoke against Moses because of the Ethiopian woman whom he had married; for he had married an Ethiopian woman. ² So they said, "Has the Lord indeed spoken only through Moses? Has He not spoken through us also? And the Lord heard it (Nu 12:1-2)."

### 4. Deborah,: The Patriotic Woman:

"Now Deborah, a prophetess, the wife of Lapidoth, was judging Israel at that time (Judges 4:4)."

### 5. Ruth,: The Woman of Constancy:

"But Ruth said: "Entreat me not to leave you, or to turn back from following after you; for wherever you go, I will go; and wherever you lodge, I will lodge; your people shall be my people, and your God, my God"(Ruth 1:16)."

### 6. Hannah,: The Ideal Mother:

"So it came to pass in the process of time that Hannah conceived and bore a son, and called his name Samuel, saying, "Because I have asked for him from the Lord" (1 Sam.1:20;2:19)."

## 7. Abigail,: The Capable Woman:

"³ The name of the man was Nabal, and the name of his wife Abigail. And she was a woman of good understanding and beautiful appearance; but the man was harsh and evil in his doings. He was of the house of Caleb" (1 Sam. 25:3,18-19)

## 8. The Shunammite,: The Hospitable Woman:

"⁸ Now it happened one day that Elisha went to Shunem, where there was a notable woman, and she persuaded him to eat some food. So it was, as often as he passed by, he would turn in there to eat some food. ⁹ And she said to her husband, "Look now, I know that this is a holy man of God, who passes by us regularly. ¹⁰ Please, let us make a small upper room on the wall; and let us put a bed for him there, and a table and a chair and a lampstand; so it will be, whenever he comes to us, he can turn in here" (2 kings 4:8-10)."

If you will notice, these women all had great influence on the men around them. These women were prominent. They were worthy of being noticed. Many women today think that, because of all that they have been through, they think they are nobody. So many women think they are insignificant. But, contrary to popular belief, God has plans for many of you because, what you think is nothing, is actually quite significant. Your life and experiences qualify you for your divine destiny and purpose. Woman of God, your order is in the fire.

# CHAPTER FIVE

## GODLY MEN OF ORDER

God is also looking for men of valor. Men that have a heart after God. God is looking for that man that will walk in the ways of God. A man that will cover his family. The husband of husbands. God is looking for a Psalm 1 man. A man that meditates on the word of God day and night. A man that walks upright. He is looking for a man that would delight himself in the laws of the Lord — one that is willing to be a man that walks in divine order. God is looking for a few good men. In Proverbs 16:7, it says that when a man's ways please the Lord, he makes even his enemies be at peace with him. Wow! That is pretty powerful. Your enemy's will be at peace with you.

### CHARACTERISTICS OF PROVERBS 31 MAN

God is looking for a man that will not give his strength to a woman, but in fact, be the strength for a woman (Proverbs 31:1-9). The man's strength comes from God. This man must be a devoted man to God. This man must not be a drunkard! Drunkenness is not for rulers and national leaders. A man that drinks could make bad decisions because his mind is not clear to make sound judgment. He must be a stable-minded man. He must not be an oppressor of men. He must not be a cruel-hearted man. This man must have a heart for the people. Heavy drinkers have been known to compromise godly principles — sometimes becoming cruel and overbearing with the people that God has entrusted them to. God is looking for a man of standard. Godly

Standards! But, in fact, still be a fair man; One that understands the ways of the Lord. A man that loves God with all of his heart, mind, and soul. A Proverbs 31 man! There are many Proverbs 31 men waiting for their orders. We need a few good men on the frontlines ready for battle. Can I get a few good men to step up to the plate and demand divine order. Men that are willing to go through the fire to receive your orders. Man of God, your order is in the fire.

## A FEW GODLY MEN

### 1. Noah, the Ark Builder:

It was divinely known to Noah that there was going to be a great flood that would destroy man from the face of the Earth because there was so much violence on the Earth. God gave Noah a strange task; a task that appeared to man to be impossible to perform. People would come to see his work and to mock him. Noah worked for many years to build the ark (Gen. 6:13). This is much like many of the things that God has called us to. Noah was obedient to what God had given him to do.

### 2. Abraham, the Father of Many Nations:

Abraham received a divine message from the Lord to separate himself from old associates and go forth into a new country. God promised Abraham divine favor, great posterity, and he would become a blessing to all the families of the Earth (Gen. 12:1-3). I remember someone asking me, "What made you move?" I thought about it for a split second, and I realized it would take too long to help someone that did not have the faith that I had to understand. So, I didn't even bother to reply.

### 3. Joseph, the Dreamer:

Joseph was a dreamer. God gave him divine revelation and all his dreams came true. He wore the coat of many colors. Joseph had divine favor of God. He resisted temptation. He saved a nation of people during the famine. Joseph was business savvy. Joseph was despised by his brothers (Gen.37:5). I am sure many of you understand that when you have a dream, you have to keep it to yourself. Your own people will hate you because God will use the very one that is the least of them. The least of them is the greatest. God will give you divine favor when you walk in divine order.

### 4. David, A Man After God's Heart:

David was Jesus' father. David committed many sins. It is unbelievable that a man that had so many great things going on was also a murderer. David killed Uriah, Bathsheba's husband. He was a fugitive. David wrote the twenty-third Psalm,: verse 1-6, along with many other psalms. When David kept the divine commandments, he had a pure heart. But, David was a man after God's heart. David was a fine musician and a poet. David had such an awesome reputation that he was sent to play for the king. He displayed powerful wisdom in the administration of government. David was a king. Today, as I look back on most of David's life, he was really no different than many of God's people. God was not looking for a perfect Christian, but in fact, looking for a man after God's heart. It is not perfection that gets God. It's endurance and a will to persevere. David was many things, but most of all he had a heart for God (1 Sam.13:14).

### 5. Solomon, A Man of (Understanding) Wisdom:

Solomon was the son of David and Bathsheba. He didn't ask for things that many people ask of God. Solomon asked God for wisdom (1 King 3:9). Solomon was anointed king before his father's death. Solomon was the richest man on the Earth. Solomon was wise beyond all men of his time. Solomon's greatest enterprise was the construction of Jerusalem. He, like many, let fame and honor go to his head. Solomon had wisdom, but he lacked self-control. In life, we must have understanding of the order of God, because without it, we have nothing. In order to have wisdom, we must have self-control. It seems strange to say that in order to have wisdom we must have self control, but the truth is, Solomon had everything he wanted, and he really didn't understand what God needed. God needs us to have divine order in order to have wisdom. God always gives us more than enough. So we have to apply the knowledge we have in order to have wisdom.

### 6. Elijah, the Prophet of Fire:

Elijah was a prototype of John the Baptist. He was rugged in his appearance and how he dressed. Elijah was known for the declarations he spoke. Each time it came to past, Elijah announced a drought. God told Elijah to go and live by the brook Cherith. During this time, Elijah depended on the ravens to supply his food. Eventually, the brook dried up and the ravens stopped feeding him. Elijah's faith was tested because, again, God commanded him to go to Zarephath. Zarephath was a famine stricken city, and it didn't look like much was coming out of there. But, God sent Elijah to the widow to be fed. Elijah gave the woman divine instruction that would bring increase to her household. During the famine, the widow's son died. Elijah prayed to God, and he stretched out his body over the boy three times. The boy was revived back to life. Elijah was the prophet of fire because he sent for Ahab, and all the 450 prophets, to meet him on Mount Carmel. Elijah told them to get a two bulls cut it into pieces. The false prophets were to lay their bull on the wood with no fire under it. Elijah also prepared his bull and put no fire under it. Elijah wanted to show the false prophets of Baal that they, their gods, were not of Abraham, Isaac, and Israel. Their gods did not answer by fire. Elijah ordered all of them to be seized and executed (1 Kings 17:23-40). At the end of the drought, Elijah prayed for rain. Elijah had many, many journeys after this mentioned. Elijah's last journey was accompanied by Elisha. Elisha asked Elijah for a double portion of his anointing. Elijah and Elisha came upon the Jordan River. He smites the water with his mantle, and the two passed over to dry ground. Elijah told Elisha, "If you see me when I am taken up, you shall have a double portion of my anointing." Suddenly, a chariot of fire appeared, and Elijah was taken up by a whirlwind into Heaven (2 Kings 2:1-11). The key here is divine order. Each time God told Elijah to do something, Elijah did it! God answers us by fire. God is a God that answers by fire. When you trust and believe what the Lord is saying, God will move by fire.

### 7. Elisha, Received a Double Portion of the Anointing:

Elisha's life mirrors that of Elijah's life. The two are twins in historical account. Elisha, like Elijah, struck the water and passed over on dry ground. Although Elisha performed many miracles that resembled the ones of Elijah, there was a difference in the two men. Elijah had periods of great depression. He never ran from his enemies, nor did he lose hope. He lived a victorious life. Elisha performed a greater number of miracles than any other prophet, except Moses. Elisha had divine grace. Christians of today, have the ability to have the same power that Elisha had. We, by faith, can perform the very same miracles. God wants us to walk in divine order to access his double portion anointing.

### 8. Daniel, the Statesman Prophet:

Daniel was highly respected by all who knew of him. Daniel had a resemblance of Joseph. Daniel, like Moses, was a statesman and a prophet. Daniel was a seer. He had a range to see which was greater than that of other prophets. Daniel, like Joseph, also worked in the king's court. Daniel's persecution would be a stepping stone to honor. His ability to interpret dreams caused him to be exalted to rulership. Daniel was an end-time prophet. God is looking for the seers of this time. There are many of you that are anointed like Daniel and walking in divine order. God is waiting to give a glimpse into the end-time. He is waiting for you to come out of the fire. You have been called for such a time as this (Esther 4:14). Once you have reached maturity, you have reached divine order. Your order is here at this point. God has chosen you to walk among great leaders (Eph.1:4).

# CHAPTER SIX

## TRIALS OF FIRE
*#1 Testimony*

This testimony will show how we have to go through many trials and tests before we reach our destiny. God showed me that it takes faith, humility, obedience, and integrity to reach our destiny. As I went through this painful experience, I realized that God was doing something within me. God used four pillars to transform my character for my divine destiny.

He was making and molding me into his servant. I attended a church where the pastor really appeared to dislike me. I really did not want to be known by anyone. I just wanted to praise and worship God 24/7. I love music. I did not like the pressures of life. I just felt so beat down because this pastor was always saying and doing mean things to me; or, so it appeared. So, I decided that I would not allow anyone to know about me. I made the decision to hide any and everything about me, and the God that I served. One day, we were all enrolling in classes, and we were encouraged to grow spiritually. Of course, I was so thirsty; I wanted all of God. I could not get enough of God. I loved God through and through. The first time I took the spiritual gifts test, it revealed that I had over eleven spiritual gifts. I went to the pastor, and he looked at me with contempt. He was angry! He told me there was no way I could have that many gifts. I didn't know what his problem was because I was operating in all of those spiritual gifts. God made sure that I operated in every one of them. I had to evangelize, witness, and bring people to salvation. I had to tell people things even when I didn't want to. I had to pray for people I didn't like. Yes, I am telling the truth. I had to lay hands on people that I really just wanted to avoid. I know right now some churchy folks are going to read this and have something to say. The truth is that they probably started out doing the very same things. This is just an example of how God made me operate in what he had given me.

I still did not want that pastor to know who I was. It was about six months later, and I had to take the spiritual gifts test again. This time though, I lied and hid some things on my spiritual gifts test. So, the pastors thought I was nobody. This was exactly what I wanted them to think. Perfect! But, I was somebody to God. I had to answer to God. Boy was that a situation! God was watching me and on my case! I was determined not to tell that pastor, or anyone for that matter, who I was; so I hid. God kept telling me, "Stop hiding who you are. I need to use you!" I thought to myself, *"They will never know. Before it's over and done, I will be long gone. They will never know anything about me."*

Finally, I took my last spiritual gifts test. I took it and God said, "This is it! You will not hide anymore!" So I took the test, and it revealed that I had the gifts of an apostle. I was gifted as a craftsman, a trailblazer, and a forerunner. I operated in all of my gifts. God kept telling me, "To whom much is given, much is required (Luke 12:48). He told me He was going to get it all. Everything He put in me, He was going to get out of me. He said He didn't care if I was eighty years old, He was going to get it all. God said, "We can do this now, while you are young, or you can be old preaching. You will fulfill the prophecy!" *Oh God,* I thought, *what does this mean?* Well, revenge is sweet! Vengeance is mine, sayeth the Lord (Romans 12:19-20). God said, "I will avenge!"

I had taken the last spiritual gifts test. And guess what? Some of the pastors of the church wanted to speak with me. You know, the ones that thought they knew everything, but nothing that really mattered. Well, guess what? Boy, were they ever wrong. I had to have a meeting with the pastors. Needless to say, it didn't go the way they thought. We sat down, and I started to tell them about themselves from the A to Z, and they were in shock. They looked like they had seen a ghost because the Lord really used me. God revealed many things about them in that meeting. God allowed me to prophesy to them. There were things revealed that only the Lord could have known. I could see the people they dealt with. Their attitude changed towards me, quickly!

Today, I understand why I had to be raised up in that atmosphere. It made me a better person because I went through so much Hell. All this came at a time when I was going through a horrible trial in my life. I was humiliated to the point that I did not even want to acknowledge who I was in God. My integrity was tested because I lied to the pastors so that they could not read my test results. My faith was tested because I had to trust God to carry me through so much pain. I had to believe God when he revealed to me who I was. And last, but not least, I had to be obedient to my Lord and Savior. Above all, I love God and I had to stop hiding who I was, because I was God's property and his servant. God is a God of order. We should never allow man to stop us from doing what is right. We should trust God to keep us in all our ways. He is the only one that can promote us (Ps.75:6-7). He takes one down and puts one up. We are to stay humbled and the Lord will promote us. Not man!

I had gotten promotion confused with control. You see, often times people in leadership try to control a situation and they have no place. Those in leadership are to be led by God. If they are not led by God, then the leadership can cause great harm to God's disciple. During this time, I was so stressed and confused. I believed that this pastor was the only way to go. But, God is the only one to whom we need to look to. Always be led by God.

## Order #1: DON'T GIVE UP AND THROW IN THE TOWEL

God revealed this to me, in Numbers 9:16-17:

"So it was always: the cloud covered it by day and the appearance of fire by night. **17** Whenever the cloud was taken up from above the tabernacle, after that the children of Israel would journey; and in the place where the cloud settled, there the children of Israel would pitch their tents."

The Lord said, "I am a cloud by day and a fire by night." What he revealed to me was this: often times, we go through trials and tests. Or, we get caught up in some type of sin, then stop to worry about what we have done. We don't forgive ourselves. We spend way too much time wallowing in self-pity. We have to throw an all-out pity party. We start feeling sorry for ourselves and blaming everyone but ourselves. We don't take responsibility for our part in the problem. When God has already forgiven us and moved on, we are still stuck in our being unforgiving. God wants us to keep up with what He has given us to do. We must forgive ourselves and move forward in what God has given us to do. Romans 8:1 — "There is therefore now no condemnation to those who are in Christ Jesus, who do not walk according to flesh, but according to the spirit." We have to keep praying and look where we are going and go forward. We have to go the way God has given us to go. God has already forgiven us of our sins. We must repent and move on. When we stay in the place of unforgiving, we are holding up the plans of God. So let's keep it moving."

In other words, keep praying, repent daily, and humble yourself so that you can keep doing whatever God has given you to do. Eccl. 7:8, (KJV) — "Better is the end of a thing than the beginning thereof: and the patient in spirit is better than the proud in spirit." Don't stop to think about what you have done. Continue to work on whatever God has given you to do. We must learn to be patient in all that we do because it is a terrible thing to rush and not know where we will end up."

I can remember just getting so upset. I would cry so hard and just give up on everything; and yes, I would even try to give up on God. I would want to give up, throw in the towel, and quit! It is funny now that I think back because, in my heart, I knew I could not give up. One reason I could not give up was because God would not allow me to quit. I was not going to allow the devil to have the upper hand in my life. God was in control!

In the beginning, God made it perfectly clear that I did not have a choice in the matter, and that I had to finish what I was called to do. Even if I backslid, God kept me on my transformational journey.

Picture this: You throw in the towel, and you are walking away. All of the sudden, the towel comes flying and hits you in the back of your head. God throws the towel right back at you. You don't have a choice. Once you have been chosen, you can't give up. You can't give in. The choice you made doesn't go away just because you decided to stop running for God. You can't quit! You have to finish the race. You can't just run away from what you are called to do. You have to endure. Endurance will help strengthen you to reach your destiny. Thousands of people are depending on you to finish what you started. People are waiting on you.

Each one of us is gifted to help someone else. When we do not complete what we start, it slows the building of the kingdom of God. You have been chosen to walk in divine order. Do not give up and throw in the towel. You have to continue to allow God to make you and mold you into the person He wants you to be. You are not your own person. You belong to God. You must process through the fire. The fire of God will bring order to your life. Pride is not of God. God will bring down the proud. When you have divine order, then you will have what it takes to receive the anointing of God. Then, God can use you. He will use you to impart to someone else. Whatever God has placed in you can be used to teach or help someone else. Each one, reach one, teach one!

Romans 8:28— "And we know that all things work together for good to those who love God, to those who are the called according to His purpose."

## ORDER #2: BEING WITH YOUR OWN KIND WILL SET IT STRAIGHT

I never understood who I was until I was obedient to God and moved to another place in time. I moved to another state and found my people on the mountain top. I was the one that everyone looked at like I was crazy because I used to praise God so hard my clothes were about to fall off. I literally, used to dance so hard that I felt like I was floating to the floor. I found order in my freedom to be who I was in God. God's anointing flowed in me, on me, and through me. God was free to do as he pleased with me because I gave my body as a living sacrifice (Romans 12:1).

The Lord had sent my friend to give me a message. She called me and said, "You have been summoned to the threshing floor." I was called to intercession. At the time, I went to the Threshing Floor Revival. I was sent to Atlanta to a church where there were a lot of prophets that worshipped and praised the Lord. This is where I met many people that were like me. I love the Lord with all my heart and mind. I can remember, during church services, we would praise God so hard the walls would sweat. We would be at church all day. When you love God and his glory is in the house, it seems like a short period of time. But, time can get away from you when you are about your Father's business. I owe it all to the glory of God.

## Order #3: TO WHOM MUCH IS GIVEN, MUCH IS REQUIRED

*(Luke 12:48)*

It is time for many of you to grow up. When I say this, I am speaking of you that are hiding and not doing what God called you to do. Sometimes, many of you never say anything, you just sit and look. You will be held accountable for what you have been given, and for what you have not used. You cannot neglect the gift inside of you (1 Timothy 4:14). You don't get to sit on your God given gifts. God will turn your life upside down to get it out of you. So hurry, because you may not have much time. Look at it like this: God gave you a gift, and you placed it on hold. God will give the assignment to someone else, if you just disregard it as if it is nothing. God took it and gave it to someone else to complete. Your time may be up! Sometimes, God gives us something to do, and it has a time limit on it. It's time to lock and load. You don't have much time. Life is a vapor (James 4:14). There are many of you in social media groups. It is sad to know that God has given you so much, and you refuse to use your gifts. When you are called home, what do you have to show? What have you done? God will ask, "What did you do with my Son? The gifts and talents that I gave you." Every one of us is given a measure. That measure is not equal to everyone else's. It is based on how God has gifted you. Some have more grace than others. To whom much is given, much is required. God is not going to want to hear your excuses. There will not be any excuses for what you don't have.

To whom much is given, much is required! Think about all that God has done for you, and you know you did not deserve it. God expects more out of you. When you are really gifted in areas that others are not, God has big plans for you. So, get yourself in order to line up with God's plans for you. What excuse do we have when God has given us all that we need to live a prosperous life? God has even promised that we will not be burned by the fire. And yet, we come so close and let fear get in the way of destiny. Knock fear out of the way and press towards the mark of the higher calling. If you love God, you will give up everything for God. So, don't lie and say you love Him, then live like a fool.

Many would say they are not stupid, yet continue to act out of stupidity, continuing to do foolish acts. Proverbs 18:2, "A fool has no delight in understanding, but in expressing his own heart." When we express our own heart this is not the heart of God. Solomon asked God for understanding, and God gave Solomon wisdom. Wisdom made Solomon one of the richness men of his time. We have not because we do not want what God has for us. Our level of intelligence is too low to comprehend what God has for us. We could be like Solomon and ask for wisdom.

In Luke 12:48, Jesus has told us how to live until he returns. We must watch for him, work diligently, and obey his commands. Such attitudes are especially necessary for leaders. Watchful and faithful leaders will be given increased opportunities and responsibilities. The more resources, talents, and understanding we have, the more we are required to use them effectively. God will not hold us responsible for gifts He has not given us, but all of us have been given enough gifts and duties to keep us busy until Jesus returns. Even though, much has been given, we still have to process through the fire to have divine order.

## ORDER #4: YOU THINK YOU MISSED IT

I would like to say this to all of you that are worried and think that you have missed it: you haven't missed anything. So relax. When it is your time, no devil in hell will be able to stop it. Every time that a door is opened, it should tell you that access is granted. Our life is a process. Some of us think we are late bloomers when in fact, there are no late bloomers. Wherever you are, is exactly where you are supposed to be. Everything you have gone through, experienced, is preparation for a future trial. God always prepares you for a process before it begins. Look at it like this, every time you go through a trial and you don't pass the test, you will repeat the test again; but with a different process but the same testing.

Continue to walk it out and stay on course. Don't fret because God has you covered. Get in the habit of being a good listener. The small things count. The process can be painful. But remember, check every area of your life to make sure that you are in the process and you are not being punished for something you have done wrong. There is a difference. Also, remember to keep that mouth shut. Complaining will delay destiny. No matter how painful it may be, don't talk about it. The enemy only knows what he hears, and complaining will set you back, too. Remember when Moses led the people out of Egypt, they murmured and complained and they stayed on that mountain for forty years. They could have been off the mountain in eleven days (Deuteronomy 1:2). The Exodus took forty years when it should have only taken eleven days! When we don't complain, we get through a test or trial much quicker. But, when we complain, the enemy knows just how and what to use against us. The revelation of this is when we are going through a struggling time. We must quickly discern what is going on with us. As soon as we realize it is a test, the better we will be.

Joshua 1:9 (NKJV) — "Have I not commanded you? Be strong and of good courage, do not be afraid, nor be dismayed, for the Lord your God is with you wherever you go." Walking through a test can be over as quickly as it starts. If we start to complain and whine, the process is extended. Like the children of Israel, if they had not complained, they would have been off that mountain much quicker. Our test would be over much quicker if we would just keep our mouths shut. No complaining, but gratitude. A test takes about a week and a half. God help us because sometimes it seems to go on for months. The irony of it is this: some of us have been carrying hurt and pain for about forty years.

## ORDER #5: GOD DON'T MAKE MISTAKES; WE DO

God is no respecter of persons. We are uniquely chosen and processed. God divinely orders our steps. We are a chosen people of royal priesthood. You see, we always get in the way. God knows exactly who he calls and chooses. We are the ones that try to put our own spin on things. When we pray, and ask God for something, God listens and He always answers us. It may not be what we want to hear, but God does answer us. We are right where we are supposed to be. We must understand that each one of us has been gifted for a particular task. It may be a small part, but everything works together for the good of God. In Romans 8:28 (NKJV)— "And we know that all things work together for good to those who love God, to those who are the called according to His purpose."

So, do not entertain thoughts that you have missed what God is doing in you. This thinking is clearly the thoughts of the enemy. Wherever you find yourself, just know that God already knew it was going to happen, or He already knew that you were going to do it before it took place. God is omniscience; He is all knowing. Our journey is sure to take us to the very places that God has designed for us to walk upon. Be at peace, for there is nothing hidden from God.

# PSALM 139

## God's Perfect Knowledge of Man

O Lord, you have searched me and known me. ² You know my sitting down and my rising up; you understand my thought afar off. ³ You comprehend my path and my lying down. And are acquainted with all my ways. ⁴ For there is not a word on my tongue, but behold, O Lord, you know it altogether.⁵ You have hedged me behind and before, and laid your hand upon me. ⁶ Such knowledge is too wonderful for me; It is high; I cannot attain it. ⁷ Where can I go from your Spirit? Or where can I flee from your presence? ⁸ If I ascend into Heaven, you are there; If I make my bed in hell, behold, you are there. ⁹ If I take the wings of the morning, and dwell in the uttermost parts of the sea, ¹⁰ Even there, your hand shall lead me, and your right hand shall hold me. ¹¹ If I say, Surely the darkness shall fall on me. Even the night shall be light about me, ¹² Indeed, the darkness shall not hide from you, but the night shines as the day; the darkness and the light are both alike to you. ¹³ For you formed my inward parts; you covered me in my mother's womb. ¹⁴ I will praise you, for I am fearfully and wonderfully made. Marvelous are your works, and that my soul knows very well. ¹⁵ My frame was not hidden from you, when I was made in secret, and skillfully wrought in the lowest parts of the Earth. ¹⁶ Your eyes saw my substance, being yet uniformed. And in your book they all were written. The days fashioned for me, when as yet there were none of them. ¹⁷ How precious also are your thoughts to me, O God! How great is the sum of them! ¹⁸ If I should count them, they would be more in number than the sand; when I awake, I am still with you. ¹⁹ Oh, that you would slay the wicked, O God! Depart from me, therefore, you bloodthirsty men. ²⁰ For they speak against you wickedly; your enemies take your name in vain. ²¹ Do I not hate them, O Lord, who hate you? And do I not loathe those who rise up against you? ²² I hate them with perfect hatred; I count them my enemies. ²³ Search me, O God, and know my heart; try me, and know my anxieties; ²⁴ And see if there is any wicked way in me, and lead me in a way everlasting.

## #2 Testimony
## Divorce

I wanted to share this because someone, somewhere is going through something similar. And, I got through this by the grace of God. God will never put more on you than you can bare.

Let me begin by saying that my marriage was rocky from the beginning because God did not ordain it. I clearly heard God say, "Do not marry him." But, love is blind. Or, should I say, "Lust is Blind." My dearly beloved had left the scene. He left everything behind, including the furniture and all the household. We struggled for a period of time, but God was always there. Today, I thank God that he was there. I lacked nothing. I prayed a lot and my home was my sanctuary. I love God more than any man on this Earth. So, when my husband left, I didn't run after him, I let him go. Today, I am grateful that I let him go. I am the woman I am today because he was not a part of God's divine plan for my life. I had to let go of my husband so that God could teach me what marriage really was about.

Marriage is a covenant between God, a husband, and a wife. I spent many days in 1 Corinthians Chapter 7. Many relationships have suffered because no one wants to take the blame for what they have done. The truth is that when a man takes a wife, they become bone of one another's bone and flesh of each other's flesh. They become one! Marriage is not conditional. Marriage is unconditional. When we take our vows, we are not planning on getting a divorce. God expects us to work on our marriage as a ministry. Many do not know, but covenant is a God-given agreement. It is until death do you part. This means staying married until you die. So, you die trying to make it better. Hopefully, you work on becoming a better person. So whatever happens to one, happens to both. God blames both of you.

So many relationships end because they do not understand covenant. Once you get married, that is it, there is no throwing in the towel because the two got into a heated argument. I am telling the truth here. As long as your partner is not abusing you physically or mentally, there is no reason for a divorce. Often times, they both say things and one or the other partner can't find the words to fight back so the offense is too much to handle. So, there goes the marriage. God is tired of the childish bickering and fighting. I thought my situation was different. My husband abandoned me with four children and married someone while he was still married to me. The question is: "Who does that?" I will tell you, a person that does not care about anyone but himself. That is all I will say about that for now. But, I do know that each waking moment is a journey. The two have to work on the marriage daily. You never really know someone. I had been married for over eighteen years, and I will say this: you think after eighteen years you would know a person. Well, it is never what you think. Marriage is a ministry. It is a journey between the two that joined together. So even in all that, God still wants us to forgive and move on. But, in all that, I give thanks to God because it showed me what I did not want in a husband. Today, I know that I am a better person for having gone through all that I went through. It is true, the best revenge is to let him or her have your mess. And that is exactly what I did. It only teaches them not to take something that did not belong to them. Anything free is not worth having, but it helped me in the process to reach my destiny. The grass is never greener on the other side.

The process I went through helped burn up everything that was not like Jesus. My order was in the fire. I was humiliated. I had to have faith to believe that God would save me from myself. I had to have integrity to do what was right in order to have obedience in God. God taught me what it took to have an intimate relationship. It also taught me to listen when God is speaking, because I remember being in prayer, and I heard God give me a scripture. At the time, I did not understand what the scripture meant. But, based on what my husband was telling me and how he was acting, it was revealed through the word of God.

The Lord gave me Luke 14:20. My husband was always telling me that he couldn't come home. Little did I know, he had married someone else while he was married to me. I had no clue until things started to unfold. So this lesson taught me to always listen to what God had to say. I would even go as far as to tell you to write things down in a journal when the Lord reveals things to you, because you may not know what it means at the time, but eventually you will come to understand clearly what the Lord is saying. When you have a pure heart and clean hands, God will reveal secret things to you. And what goes on in the dark will come to the light.

# CHAPTER SEVEN

## FOUR AREAS OF TESTING:

## FAITH

*Hebrews 11:1 – "Now faith is the substance of things hoped for, the evidence of things not seen."*

Faith is inviting God's Holy Spirit to live within us. It is not just an act of the mind; it taps us into the resources of God so that we have the power to live in an entirely new way. If God himself is living within us, our lives should be dramatically changed.

God will really test your faith when he asks you to do something and you don't see how you will accomplish it. Anyone who walks with God will find his faith tested. You have to trust God completely. Faith without works is dead. We have to work on the task of being in divine order daily. God gives us a mission to complete, and we get caught up in the worldly things and forget to keep the faith and complete what God has given us to do. We have to have faith to believe what God tells us before we can hold on to what we believe. When we hold on to faith we will have the ability to finish what God has given us. Faith is a gift from God. It is a divine ability to hold onto divine order.

Faith will cause us to finish the task at hand. Believe that God can work His plan through your life. Believe that He will mightily work through you. In this dispensation, you only have to believe to receive. "All things are possible" (Mark 9:23). God will do abundantly above all that you can ask. You only have to believe (Ephesians 3:20). Dare to believe and nothing will be impossible for you (Matt. 17:20).

When you are going through tests and trials, you must count it all joy. You must have faith to "know that you know that you know" (Wigglesworth).

## #3 Testimony

God tested me in the area of faith by telling me to give up everything and move from North Carolina. There were many miracles, signs, and wonders to give evidence that it was, in fact, God. I had an Abraham experience. I left my career with the Department of Defense. I had been employed there for seventeen and a half years. I gave up the home that I had just acquired through my divorce. I listened to God, and I moved to Atlanta, Georgia. I trusted God for everything. I had no family or friends in Georgia. I had no one but God. God is El Shaddai. He is more than enough. You just need faith to believe.

2 Corinthians 5:7— "For we walk by faith, not by sight." I could not go by what I saw or felt. I kept my eyes on God. I am not saying that it was easy. I am telling you that I trusted God with what seemed impossible. God provided everything I needed. God opened doors that no man could open. My children and I moved, and we started over in a place where no one knew us. The one thing I noticed was that it felt like I was supposed to be there, and I had no worries of how I would survive.

In Galatians 3:14, the Bible tells us that the blessings of Abraham have come upon the Gentiles by faith. What does this mean? First, we must know Abraham. Abraham was the father of faith. In Genesis 12:1, God called Abram and his family to leave his country and away from his kinsman, and told him to go to a land that He (God) would show him. When I got to Georgia, I didn't know anyone. It was all new to me.

Something like this could be very frightening. I left the familiar behind. I left the soul ties and the past behind. I was starting anew and fresh.

So many times we move from the past and carry the old baggage with us. Abraham left the past and the familiar things behind. In order to do this, Abraham had to have a ridiculous amount of faith to accomplish. God made Abraham a promise in verse 2 and 3. Look at Genesis 12:2-3. This blessing on Abraham's life would cause situations, circumstances, finances, people, and even nations to kneel before him. God spoke a blessing over Abraham's life. Whomever God blesses, no one can curse. I did this, and I have been blessed beyond anything I could have ever imagined. Obedience is what it takes.

When we believe and trust God, we can do anything, we are operating in faith. We must press in and pray as if we already have what we are asking for. You really have to just know, without doubt, that God is going to do it. There should be no doubt that God can and will do what he said he would do. If you are going through something that is so massive and you feel as though you have little or no faith, just know that, if God said it, believe it. God is faithful. He always keeps his promises. Look at Moses when he took the children of Israel and crossed the Red Sea. Noah built the Ark that housed an entire population to start the beginning of the new world. Jonah was eaten by a whale and he was in the whale's belly for three days. I could go on, but you get the understanding of what I am telling you.

Faith is an area that God tested me in so that I would get in place to reach my destiny. So, for many of you that God has told to move and you are still sitting there, you have been disobedient. Disobedience falls in line with rebellion, witchcraft, distrust, ignorance, disbelief, being a liar, broke mentality, little faith, or no prayer.

If God brings you to it, He will see you through it. But, God has to test us in the area of faith to see if we can be trusted with the next level of anointing before He places it on us. Did you know that if you don't believe, then you don't receive? If you don't believe it, it's like you don't want a blessing. Start believing so you can receive it. "Faith comes from hearing, and hearing through the word of Christ" (Romans 10:17, ESV). Sometimes, we have to be tried more than once, but we eventually pass the test. Be like Nike, just do it. We are our own worst enemy. We make excuses. Just do it. Trust God! Don't stop to think about it; just do what God told you to do. God knows what is best for you. Kick fear to the curb. Walk and run with faith.

We are called to persevere. Transformation will build your faith. Hebrews 10:19-23 (NIV)— "Therefore, brothers, since we have confidence to enter the Most Holy Place by the blood of Jesus, [20] by a new and living way opened for us through the curtain, that is, his body, [21] and since we have a great priest over the house of God, [22] let us draw near to God with a sincere heart in full assurance of faith, having our hearts sprinkled to cleanse us from a guilty conscience and having our bodies washed with pure water. [23] Let us hold unswervingly to the hope we profess, for he who promised is faithful."

We must draw near to God so that we may grow in faith, overcome our doubts, and develop a deeper relationship with God. A stronger relationship is where our faith grows stronger. Stronger faith is where obedience is strengthened.

## OBEDIENCE

### *Letter From God*

My child, how long will you deceive me? Do you not know that deception is witchcraft? Do not come to me with filth. Zechariah 1:3, "Therefore say to them, '"Thus' says the Lord of hosts, '"Return to me', says the Lord of hosts, " 'and I will return to you'," says the Lord of hosts." 'Of course, I will forgive you. But, I will not forget your dishonor. You shall reap what you have sown'.". Galatians 6:7, "Do not be deceived, God is not mocked; for whatever a man sows, that he will also reap. 8 For he who sows to his flesh will of the flesh reap corruption, but he who sows to the Spirit will of Spirit reap everlasting life."

There are many waiting for what I have placed in your belly. I will remove what I have given you and replace it with the void that you have already requested. You do not want me. You would rather live for this world, than to live for the kingdom that awaits you. You rob me daily with deception and tricks of the enemy. You are not your own. You belong to me. I am your God! You prefer the worldly kingdoms over the kingdom of God. The kingdom of God is more powerful than the kingdoms of this world. Yet, you are confused and you continue to take the broad path. The road that leads to many paths, highways, and roads that lead to death. Your path has no place in my kingdom. The stench of yesterday still radiates from your inner being. There is no glow from Heaven. No deposit into your heavenly accounts. Just smoke from the stench of burning bowels. Romans 6:23, "For the wages of sin is death, but the gift of God is eternal life in Christ Jesus our Lord." We are free to choose between two masters: sin or Christ Jesus. The wages of sin is eternal death. That is all you can expect or hope for in life without God. By choosing Christ as your master, you receive his gift of eternal life - new life with God that begins on Earth and continues forever with God. What choice have you made? Don't you know, the wages of sin is death! Repent, for your kingdom of darkness is soon to undertake you and all that is near to you. There is only one true living God. Yet, you dishonor me. Are you hot, cold, or lukewarm? I would prefer that you be hot, but you have chosen to be lukewarm. Revelation 3:16, "So then, because you are lukewarm and neither cold nor hot, I will vomit you out of my mouth."

You may think to yourself, I have time. I am young! Time waits for no one. James 4:14, "Whereas you do not know what will happen tomorrow. For what is your life? It is even a vapor that appears for a little time and then vanishes away." God is the only one with time in his hand. Psalm 31:15, "My times are in your hand; deliver me from the hand of my enemies, and from those that persecute me." The Lord is urging you to come out from them. 2 Corinthians 6:17, "Therefore, come out from amongst them, and be separate, says the Lord. Do not touch what is unclean, and I will receive you."

Chose this day whom you shall serve. Joshua 24:14, "Now therefore, fear the Lord, serve Him in sincerity and in truth, and put away the gods which your fathers served on the other side of the river and in Egypt. Serve the Lord. 15 "and if it seems evil to you to serve the Lord, choose for yourselves this day whom you will serve, whether the gods which your fathers served that were on the other side of the river, or gods of the Amorites, in whose land you dwell. But as for me and my house, we will serve the Lord."

My child I urge you return to your first love before it is too late. Jeremiah 31:3, "The Lord has appeared of old to me, saying, '"Yes I have loved you with an everlasting love; therefore with loving-kindness I have drawn you'" REPENT, REPENT, REPENT!!! Matthew 3:2, "And saying, Repent, for the kingdom of Heaven is at hand!" Isaiah 40:3, "For this is he who was spoken of by the Prophet Isaiah saying, 'the voice of one crying in the wilderness. Prepare the way of the Lord; make his paths straight!'" Thus say the Lord."

\*\*\*\*

God is looking for those that He can trust with what He has placed in us. Obedience is key to access the anointing. God has to test us to see if we will believe and trust Him. Many, out of fear, do not trust God. Or you are just plain rebellious. Some people lie to God as if God is stupid. God already knows who He can trust with His anointing. So, the reality here is this: God calls the ones that He already knows will be obedient to what He has asked of them. This is why so many people are faking their anointing. The power of the anointing is in the obedience.

We have to do it God's way, not our way. Jeremiah 29:11, paraphrase, "God knows the plans He has for us. These plans are for good and not of disaster, to give us a future and a hope." Once you have come to understand obedience, then you will understand the difference between obedience and disobedience. The Lord will teach you right from wrong. The chosen ones are forbidden to do what everyone else is doing. God will set you apart. Set apart means Holy.

## HUMILITY

Do not think because God is going to bless you, that you won't go through anything. You need to humble yourself to receive the blessing. You have to be tested to get to the promise. Proverbs 18:12 — "Before destruction the heart of a man is haughty, and before honor is humility." Many times we experience some things that are truly horrible. There is always a sunny side after we go through darkness. Humility will cause you to be broken. God breaks us before we can receive any type of honor. Proverbs 22:4 — "By humility and the fear of the Lord are riches and honor and life." When God breaks us, it keeps us humble, you will keep running back to God. True humility and fear of the Lord leads to riches, honor, and long life.

A broken spirit is a humble spirit. You will never forget God as long as you are humbled in humility. Proverbs 29:23 — "A man's pride will bring him low, but the humble in spirit will retain honor." Pride will end in humiliation, while humility brings honor. We are tested in humility daily. Each test is designed to pull up some stuff hidden in your flesh. You should repent daily. As we walk in a humbled state of mind, we will not get ahead of ourselves. Isaiah 57:15 — "For thus says the High and Lofty One who inhabits eternity, whose name is Holy: I dwell in the high and holy place, with him who has a contrite and humble spirit, to revive the heart of the contrite ones." Glory to God! God has to reveal what is in you before He covers you. He gives honor to those with a repentant heart. It was better for me to humble myself and be obedient to what God was asking me to do. I had to be childlike, instead of being childish. Matthew 18:4 — "Therefore, whoever humbles himself as this little child is the greatest in the kingdom of Heaven."

The hidden purpose of destruction had to be exposed. God had to expose the good, the bad, and the ugly. He had to expose the purpose of His glory to rest in you, on you, and through you. Expose Himself (God) in you. 1 Peter 4:12 — "Beloved, do not think it strange concerning the fiery trial which is to try you, as though some strange thing happened to you." Every time God gives you a promise you must be tried and tested to qualify to receive the promise.

## #4 Testimony

The one thing you think God will not do is what He will do to you to break you and to use you. Humility will make you feel horrible, but is good for your soul. It was better for me to humble myself and be obedient to what God was asking me to do. I had to be childlike, instead of being childish.

God made me minister to my ex-husband even though he had left me and our children. I was still married to him at the time, and I had no choice but to minister to him to receive salvation. I was hurting, but I had to be tested in this area for a humbling experience. This was the last thing I wanted to do, but I did it. God asked me to bring my husband to salvation. My response was, "Are you serious? Can't you get somebody else to do this?" Now, before you nail me to a cross, I am being honest. I didn't want anything to do with him. This was so humiliating. I was hurting so bad. My husband had abandoned my children and I, but God told me 'yes'! He said, "I chose you to bring him into the kingdom of God because you are the closest to him." I was the only one that could do it because I was responsible for him. I was married to him.

This will help a whole lot of people right here. When you marry, you are responsible until death do you part. He was still my husband. Some of you women are wondering why you can't get past the old stuff. Pray and close that chapter in your life, release that old mess. My humility was so that I would be broken in spirit to cause me to have clean hands and a contrite spirit (Psalm 51:17). Forgiveness is required to humble yourself. The Lord needed me to walk in humility in order to draw my ex-husband so that he would receive salvation. Romans 12:3, (NKJV)— "For I say, through the grace given to me, to everyone who is among you, not to think of himself more highly than he ought to think, but to think soberly, as God has dealt to each one a measure of faith."

You see, I did not want to minister to my ex-husband because I was angry, and I was judging him because of all the wrong he had done. And the Lord let me know that I was no better than him because we were one. I really did not want to hear this, but I submitted to God and was obedient to what God was telling me to do. I had to remember that it wasn't about me, but about Jesus Christ. I humbled myself under God, and in the process, I was truly blessed. Even though we did not get back together, I learned a very powerful lesson. God gives grace to the humble (1 Peter 5:5). As I humbled myself, he was drawn and he received salvation from the Lord.

When you walk in humility, people can see that you are trustworthy. People can see that you are willing to sacrifice for the grace of God. Pride will keep you from doing what is right. When we humble ourselves it allows us to get closer to God. And it also brings order and honor to our lives.

## INTEGRITY

Job 2:3, "Then the Lord said to Satan, 'Have you considered my servant Job, that there is none like him on the Earth, a blameless and upright man, one who fears God and shuns evil?' And still he holds fast to his integrity, although you incited me against him to destroy him without cause."

Everyone is not blameless and upright. It is a matter of doing the right thing. When you keep your word, this is a sign of integrity. Faithfulness is another sign of integrity. The question is, have you done everything right?

God will test you in the area of integrity to see if you are walking in divine order. Integrity is a must-have to reach your divine destiny. God will test you in many areas of integrity. Many people go shopping and when they take their grocery carts to the parking lot, they do not return them to the stall. Or, when we check out our groceries and get to the car only to realize there are still unpaid items in the cart. The integral thing would be to return these items to the store or their rightful place, immediately. I know that it can be a headache to get all the way up front, after all of your shopping is done, and find out that there is an item you do not want in your shopping basket. You may be tempted to leave it on a nearby shelf, but you should go all the way back and place it on the shelf where you originally picked it up. Put it back where it belongs. Or sometimes the cashier will give back too much change. Give it back because later on, at the close of business, that cashier's cash drawer will come up short of cash. That cashier could be fired and lose everything because of someone being untruthful. Even when you find someone's purse, please just return it. Do the right thing so that God can and will do right by you. God is watching. You will be thankful that you did the right thing.

Integrity is a characteristic that many of God's people do not have. You must have integrity in order to serve God's people. You must be faithful and committed to serving God's people. People are depending on God's servants to be dependable and trustworthy. We must be integral in character before we can serve God. If you can't serve God, then you certainly will not be able to serve his people.

There are many things that God expects of us. Integrity is very important to God. One thing for sure is that, if you are a liar, you cannot serve God fully. So, if you have been in the habit of being a liar, you should stop telling people things you do not mean. Do what you say you are going to do. Otherwise, you are a liar. Learn to be a man or woman of your word. No one likes a liar. Satan is the father of lies (John 8:44). Also, pay your tithes because you may think it doesn't matter, but give honor to God, not people. Respect God by respecting his servants. Leave the finger pointing to God. Trust God with the tithe. The money doesn't belong to you anyway. Everything we have belongs to God. God is not slack in what he sees and does not see.

Integrity is not just doing what you say you will do, but also taking time to make sure that everything is in order so that there is no question as to whether or not you have good character. An integral person leaves nothing to chance. Consistency is another sign that you are an integral person. It lets people know that you will complete the task at hand. When people look and see consistency, they expect nothing less of you. Psalm 25:21 – "Let integrity and uprightness preserve me, for I wait for you." There are two forces needed to preserve us along life's way; they are integrity and honesty. Honesty makes us understand God's requirements and strive to fulfill them. Integrity tells others that you will walk consistently in it. Proverbs 11:3 – "The integrity of the upright will guide them, but the perversity of the unfaithful will destroy them."

People can trust and know that you are a man or woman of your word. An integral person is a person that does not waver in their decisions. There will be no compromising. You won't cut corners to get things done. You'll do things the safe way. Cheating shows a lack of integrity. Cheaters never win. Proverbs 19:1 – "Better is the poor who walk in his integrity than one who is perverse in his lips, and is a fool." Many people are afraid of not getting what they want. They will pay any price to increase their wealth. So, they cheat and steal from others, cheating on their taxes, stealing from stores or employers, withholding tithes, refusing to give. When we know and love God, we realize that a lower standard of living is a small price to pay for personal integrity. When you pay the price, God will give you the anointing. Proverbs 20:7— "The righteous man walks in his integrity; his children are blessed after him." When you walk upright, even your offspring will be blessed.

Many folks think God is a "sugar daddy". When they pray, they just want stuff. No one wants to pay the price to receive what the Lord has for them. I say this: stop asking God for things that you already know you are not going to pay for. You say you want more of God, but you don't even know what you are asking God for. The songs you sing in church, often times, are being sung to God. When we sing, we worship God. So, here you are singing songs telling God, "Give me more of you." God knows and understands worship. Now, He wants to give you what you ask for. But first, what are you going to give me? What are you going to do for me? Are you going to serve me?

Many are frustrated because they cannot get things from God. And all you see is pain and so much going through. Excuse my improper language, but God ain't stupid! God is not going to just give you what you ask for. There needs to be order in your life. You need to make some preparations to receive what you are asking God for. Trust me, when you get what you are asking for, you will not want it. It will come with a price. Anointing is not free. It's earned through a process. You have to work for it. It comes through pain. It is a process birthed through pain. My anointing was birthed through many levels of pain. God wants you to walk in divine order, but you have to walk out the process.

People are so busy adding their mess to what God has for them. God is a God of order. So many people think that repetition and tradition are of God. It is nothing, but religiosity. Submit to God! Come all the way in. Give up your own personal agenda. Let God reveal himself to you, so that you know that religious acts are not of God. Learn to have a kingdom agenda. Just because this is the way that Pastor Knowsbest did it, this way does not make it right. God is not a sugar daddy! You can't just go into prayer and start asking God for stuff. When you ask for stuff, this is your own selfish agenda. How can you ask for something when you have not given God anything?

Oh sure, I see the pastor's anniversary, the pastor's conference, the birthday parties, and the children's plays. Let me be honest, what does any of this have to do with the kingdom of God? Of course, it doesn't! No witnessing to the people in your immediate circle of friends. For that matter, witness to that wayward family member, feed the homeless, help the widows in the church, and nobody got saved during these events. The only thing people are looking for is a favorite spot in the pastor's heart. Oh, don't let me forget the prosperity messages that so many pastors are preaching these days. They just want your money. Yeah, I said it. Just mess! Religiosity at its finest! Correct me if I am wrong, but this is not the sign of integrity.

Integrity is doing the right thing when no one is watching. God did not call you, sanctify you, or summons you to serve yourself, but instead to serve God's people. So many times we see that integrity is no longer the thing to do. But now, it's 'do what everybody else is doing'. People just do it, whether it is right or wrong.

Women, if you know God and He has given you an understanding of Him, then you need to go and check on these single women and their children. Men, teach these other men how to be men and survive. Teach them how to war in the Heavenlies for their families. Don't just feed the homeless— take them and rehabilitate them. Minister to those people to get their understanding about Jesus.

John 3:30— "He must increase, but I must decrease. We must do what God has told us to do and be in the order of God." God is a God of order. God is looking for an integral people. When we do it God's way, then that is all that needs to be done. There is always a way that seems right, but it ends wrong. Proverbs 14:12— "There is a way that seems right to man, but its end is the way of death." The way that seems right may offer many options and require few sacrifices. The right choice often requires hard work and self-sacrifices. Don't take shortcuts because they might end in terrible consequences. No extra stuff; just God's way.

John 3:31— "He who comes from above is above all. He who is of the Earth is earthly and speaks of the Earth. He who comes from Heaven is above all." Our words should only be about Jesus. We should have a Heavenly persona. The traditions of man have nothing to do with God. Jesus spoke nothing but the truth. When people put their ideas and meaningless thoughts into action, it becomes religiosity. People are no longer thinking about Jesus. They are not doing things God's way, but in fact, they now have their own agenda. 1 Kings 18:24— "Then you call on the name of your gods, and I will call on the name of the Lord; and the God who answers by fire, He is God." So, all the people answered and said, '"It is well spoken.'" Many people don't realize it, but having your own agenda is creating your own gods. The Lord God Almighty is the only one true living God.

The fire of God will burn up anything that is not like Him. Have you ever wondered why things just seem to be going right, then all the sudden start going wrong? Well, that is because God is a God that judges the wrongdoings of man. We cannot reach our destiny if we are out of order. We need to incorporate the kingdom of God in our daily lives. We need to live by the ways of God. God is all that we will ever need. The Lord is the God that answers by fire. God breathes on your situation to turn it around. God speaks to us in our dreams. When it is quiet, the Lord will come to you and He will tell you things. The thing to do is to listen to what He says to do. God is a just God. Listen to what He is telling you and don't share it.

Often times, sharing is not the integral thing to do, because if God wanted you to share, He would tell you to share it. Otherwise, keep your mouth shut. I know it can be exciting to hear what the Lord is saying, but it can also be detrimental, as well. Your information can be shared with the wrong person and it could become a loss. You share, the next person shares, and it becomes gossip. Learn to keep the things that God gives you to yourself. God is infinite in His being. He does not need your help. He just needs you to do what He told you to do. Integrity will take you to your next level. Integrity is a part of God's consuming fire. When you have integrity, you have the order of God.

## #5 Testimony

God will always be with you as long as you are living an integral life. When you keep your eyes on God, He will show you the right things to do. God will keep no good thing from you. Nothing will be hidden from you.

Luke 8:17— "For nothing is secret that will not be revealed, nor anything hidden that will not be known and come to light." Everything that is wrong will be revealed. When light shines on darkness, all untruth is revealed. That is why the truth is the light. God revealed what was hidden in my life.

God will reveal the things that are hidden if we wait long enough. God is faithful! This is why it is so important that we be people of integrity, because God will expose your unfaithfulness over time. Nothing is hidden from God. Especially, if you are a man or woman of God that is seeking God with your whole heart. God will leave nothing to chance. He will reveal the truth of the matter. He wants every area of our lives to be made whole and complete. He will show you the hidden things that you need to know in order to walk in integrity to get to your divine destiny.

# IN CONCLUSION

You cannot do anything without God. You must pray about everything all the time. When you believe what you are praying about, then you will receive it. This is what brings everything full circle. As a peculiar people, God has ordered our steps. God will give you direction. When our ways are pleasing to the Lord, He will be with us every step of the way in our process. You have to trust God and don't give up and throw in the towel. God has a plan for your destiny. Everyone has a plan for a divine destiny.

People are so much like the men and women of the Biblical times. People never really change; they just change what they are doing. There is a remnant of men and women that have characteristics of divine order. God wants us to take what He has given us and use it to perform miracles. Your order is in the fire! Divine order is the key to releasing God's miracles.

Sometimes, God has to take us through some painful experiences. Often times, we have to be tested and retested for purification and sanctification. God has to know that He can truly trust you with the fire. You are not alone. God is always just a prayer away. He has given you everything you need to do what He has assigned you to do. Every gift that God has given you is designed to place you before great and mighty men (Proverbs 18:16). There are no mistakes when we are gifted for our anointing. God wants us to understand the key points that will cause His anointing to rest on you. The key points to anointing are faith, obedience, humility, and integrity. When we are processed in these areas, God will release His anointing and pour out his spirit on all of us (Acts 2:17).

You need to repent for being out of order. Pray that God forgive you for not lining up with the order of God. Ask God to forgive you of your disobedience. Then, let God really process you. You must allow God to go deep, to the core of your spirit, and break up every little bit of self that is blocking God from being Himself in you. God has to purge you and mold you at the same time. When God purges you, He will burn up everything that is not of Him. You need a pure, repenting heart, so that you are walking in right standing. He wants us to stop asking for stuff. God gives us everything we need daily. I pray that this book will cause you to run after God and be on fire for God. So many decisions to be made. Just tell God, YES!

Psalm 68:19, "Blessed be the Lord who daily loads us with benefits. The God of our salvation!" Instead of asking for stuff, try asking God what you can do for Him. The Lord really wants to give you more of what you need, so that He can use you.

Repent from all ungodly sin. 2 Chronicles 7:14— "If my people, who are called by my name, will humble themselves and pray and seek my face and turn from their wicked ways, then I will hear from Heaven, and will forgive their sin and heal their land." I believe that God is talking to you. The ones that He has called to ministry. Repent and let God process you in the following areas: humility, obedience, faith, and integrity; then you will hear God calling you to a higher level of anointing. The order of God is waiting for you to make the right move.

Jesus is coming soon. You don't have much time to get in order. He wants to give you your orders. He wants to summon you to bring order. He's waiting for you. He is calling you! He's waiting for you to put things in divine order. Come walk into your divine destiny. Seek God about the things He has given you to do. Do what God told you to do.

~Your Order Is In The Fire~

**BEFORE THE FIRE IS LIT, YOU MUST GATHER THE KINDLING; THE STRUGGLE IGNITES THE BLAZE. THE BLAZE INCREASES AS THE MOMENTUM BUILDS. SUDDENLY, THE FIRE IS LIT AND THE ORDER IS READY!**

*~Apostle Lisa Exum*

## Prayer

Lord, help me to do your will, your way. Give me endurance to complete my destiny. Restore me, heal me, make me whole. Impart in me the strength to walk in divine order. I decree and declare that I shall walk in my divine destiny. In Jesus' name Amen!

# DEFINITIONS

**Dispensation** - a word used to identify the unique economy of the Lord's kingdom. Dispensation means stewardship, administration, management, and oversight of another's property. *The Prophet's Dictionary, The Ultimate Guide to Supernatural Wisdom. Paula A. Price, PH.D.Whitaker House.1999,2002,2006.*

**Fool** - A silly or stupid person. Stupid is defined as: lacking intelligence.

**Kabod** - In addition to the word identifying the overwhelming brilliance and awe brought on by the appearance of God's presence, it is the Hebrew word for glory used in the Bible. Kabod describes the excellence and the power of the Lord's presence and anointing bestowed on people. Glory was, by definition, meant to be weighty, demanding, and empowering endowment of the Highest God. It was a necessary enabler for anyone to do anything for the Lord. The bestowing of God's glory immediately sanctified the person for His proximate use. It elevated them in stature and position in the kingdom, and once bestowed, attracted a host of benefits, blessings, honors, and privileges. *The Prophet's Dictionary, The Ultimate Guide to Supernatural Wisdom. Paula A. Price, PH.D.Whitaker House.1999,2002,2006.*

**Prostrate** - to lay (oneself)face down on the ground, as in humility.

**Realm** - a royal domain; kingdom. *Webster Concise Dictionary, 2d., 1997.*

# ABOUT THE AUTHOR

Apostle Lisa Exum is a modern day apostle. Her strong apostolic and prophetic background abilities as seer/prophetess, and teacher give her the ability to focus on building God's people through equipping, empowerment, motivation, and mobilization. Her powerful strategies promote discipline, healing, and deliverance. She is a visionary aimed at developing leaders globally, through training and mentoring the Body of Christ for God's kingdom and purpose. Apostle Lisa Exum is the founder of Women of Divine Destiny, Inc. She is that Woman on The Mountain!!

She holds master degrees in Health Service Administration and Public Administration from Central Michigan University, and Master of Divinity from Liberty Theological Seminary. She is world known and respected throughout the United States and overseas in many nations. She resides in Atlanta, Georgia.

If you are interested in being mentored by Apostle Lisa Exum feel free to email me: www.womenofdivinedestiny1@gmail.com or website: www.womenofdivinedestiny.com

www.ingramcontent.com/pod-product-compliance
Lightning Source LLC
Chambersburg PA
CBHW071541080526
44588CB00011B/1748